from the library of

_____

the BIG GAY Alphabet COLORING BOOK

JACINTA BUNNELL
& LEELA CORMAN

The Big Gay Alphabet Coloring Book
Jacinta Bunnell & Leela Corman

ISBN: 9781629630922
Library of Congress Control Number: 2015930880

Design: Serena Rodriguez & Jacinta Bunnell

queerbookcommittee.com

❋

PM Press
PO Box 23912
Oakland, CA 94623
pmpress.org

Reach & Teach
144 W. 25th Avenue
San Mateo, CA 94403
reachandteach.com

Printed in the USA on recycled paper

DEDICATION

This book is dedicated to my elementary school teachers.

During their tenure at Waverly Elementary School, they lovingly taught hundreds of children the many various ways one can be devoted to the alphabet and to crayons. They changed my life with their kindness, crafts, extra dittos, sparkling-eyed laughter, dolphin-themed puppet shows, and belief that each child has something special to offer the world. It is not easy being a teacher in a broken system. School is not the answer for everyone, but it was for me. It was there that I found direction, stability, a passion for letters, and at least one big gay role model.

—Jacinta Bunnell

INTRODUCTION

The Big Gay Alphabet Coloring Book illustrates twenty-six words that highlight memorable victories, collective moments, and ordinary schemes in LGBTQP (lesbian, gay, bisexual, transgender, queer, questioning, and pansexual) culture. We invite you to take your crayons out of your holsters and embark on a fantastical journey inside this book, to a place where everyone knows at least one downy unicorn and wakes up to find glitter on the soles of their slippers in the sparingly lit hours of the morning. As you add your own extraordinary colors to these pages, we hope you are left asking, "Isn't everything fabulous in this world just a little bit gay?" This book celebrates this notion on every unique page.

Each day, we take another step toward a greater understanding of gender fluidity, gender diversity, and sexual orientation. Change does not come easily or unfold overnight. But together we are an enduring and dedicated squad of comrades staring down oppression until it melts under our unwavering, unmasked gaze, stopping periodically to feel ecstatic gratefulness for the lives we are living among some purely exquisite and passionate souls.

You are a fetching mythical animal, a precious gem, as brilliant and radiant as the stars. Thank you for being you and inviting us to be part of your world. This is our zeitgeist.

GAY *(adjective)*: bright and attractive, cheerful, happily excited, keenly alive, exuberant, having or inducing high spirits, lively, given to social pleasures.

GAY *(adjective)*: of, relating to, or having a sexual orientation to persons of the same gender. Colloquial term used as an umbrella meant to include all lesbian, gay, bisexual, transgender, queer, questioning, and pansexual (LGBTQP) people.

Synonyms: gleeful, merry, keen, animated, rollicking, spirited, light-hearted, joyous, jolly, sunny, lively, zippy, sparkling, whimsical, frolicsome, chipper, playful, glittering, vivacious, confident, fun-loving, resilient, extraordinary, debonair, devil-may-care

Antonyms: ordinary, joyless, depressed, colorless, lifeless, plain, dull, sad, discouraged, overburdened, long-suffering, cheerless, lethargic, worried, lackadaisical, spiritless

A
Astrology

The Big Gay Alphabet Coloring Book

Beaches

City Hall

Double Dating

Earmuffs

The Big Gay Alphabet Coloring Book

Football

Glitter

The Big Gay Alphabet Coloring Book

Hula Hooping

I

Ice Cream

Jazz Hands

K

Karaoke

L

Leotards

Musicals

N

Narwhals

Opera

Puppets

Queens

The Big Gay Alphabet Coloring Book

Rainbows

Soul Train

T

Trapeze

U

Unicorns

V

Vampires

Weightlifting

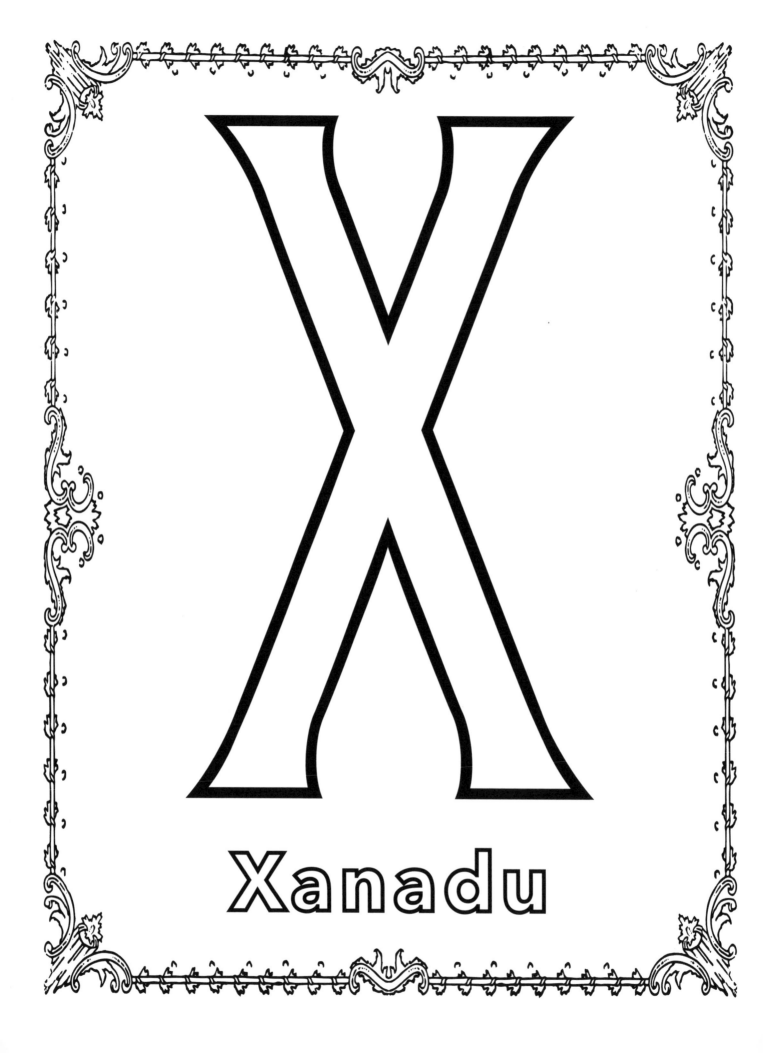

Xanadu

Y

You

Zeitgeist

Name _____ Standing and Advancement for the Year Beginning _____

PROGRESS REPORT AND PROMOTION CERTIFICATE

Study Categories	Percentage in Various Branches			
	①	②	③	④
observes, investigates, and experiments with accuracy				
colors outside the lines with focus and intent				
shares book with friends and works well with others				
shows pride in abilities				
asks for help from trusted companions				
shows growth in problem-solving abilities				
shows originality in thinking and expression				
develops new coloring techniques				
shows active interest in the world around				
works for the good of self and others				
grows understanding and appreciation of how and why others live as they do				
accepts responsibility for the improvement of human relations				
listens with thought, interest, and respect to others				
uses knowledge attained from this book in daily living				
cooperates with community of others to add beauty to the surrounding world				
develops critical understanding of the alphabet				

Explanation of marks:

achievement supervisor

This is Jacinta Bunnell's fourth coloring book in the collection known as the Queerbook Committee. Jacinta is an artist who cofounded a philanthropic fancy-costumed ladies' arm wrestling league in the Hudson Valley. She lives among some very debonair coyotes, bears, rabbits, unicorns, humans, zinnias, and rhododendron bushes.

Leela Corman is the author and illustrator of *Queen's Day* and *Unterzakhn*. Leela is an instructor and performer of Middle Eastern dance. She is a cofounder of the Sequential Artists' Workshop, a nonprofit organization dedicated to the prosperity and promotion of comic art in Gainesville, Florida, where she is also an instructor at the University of Florida.

GIRLS ARE NOT CHICKS
Coloring Book
Jacinta Bunnell & Julie Novak
$10.00

Thirty-six pages of feminist fun! This is a coloring book you will never outgrow. *Girls Are Not Chicks* is a subversive and playful way to examine how pervasive gender stereotypes are in every aspect of our lives. This book helps to deconstruct the homogeneity of gender expression in children's media by showing diverse pictures that reinforce positive gender roles for girls.

Color the Rapunzel for a new society. She now has power tools, a roll of duct tape, a Tina Turner album, and a bus pass!

Paint outside the lines with Miss Muffet as she tells that spider off and considers a career as an arachnologist!

Girls are not chicks. Girls are thinkers, creators, fighters, healers, and superheroes.

"An ingeniously subversive coloring book." —Heather Findlay, Editor in Chief, *Girlfriends* magazine

"Get this cool feminist coloring book even if you don't have a kid." —Jane Pratt, *Jane* magazine

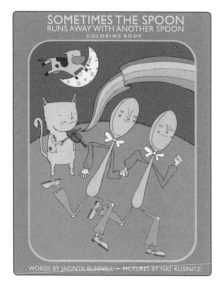

SOMETIMES THE SPOON RUNS AWAY WITH ANOTHER SPOON
Coloring Book
Jacinta Bunnell & Nathaniel Kusinitz
$10.00

We have the power to change fairy tales and nursery rhymes so that these stories are more realistic. In *Sometimes the Spoon Runs Away with Another Spoon* you will find anecdotes of real kids' lives and true-to-life fairy tale characters. This book pushes us beyond rigid gender expectations while we color fantastic beasts who like pretty jewelry and princesses who build rocket ships.

Celebrate sensitive boys, tough girls, and others who do not fit into a disempowering gender categorization.

Sometimes the Spoon Runs Away with Another Spoon aids the work of dismantling the Princess Industrial Complex by moving us forward with more honest representations of our children and ourselves. Color to your heart's content. Laugh along with the characters. Write your own fairy tales. Share your own truths.

"The children's coloring book for young princes who yearn for a knight in shining armor." —*Queerty*

"As moving and funny as *Walter the Farting Dog*." —Ayun Halliday, *East Village Inky*

FRIENDS OF PM PRESS
MONTHLY SUBSCRIPTION PROGRAM

These are indisputably momentous times—the financial system is melting down globally and the Empire is stumbling. Now more than ever there is a vital need for radical ideas.

In the seven years since its founding—and on a mere shoestring—PM Press has risen to the formidable challenge of publishing and distributing knowledge and entertainment for the struggles ahead. With hundreds of releases to date, we have published an impressive and stimulating array of literature, art, music, politics, and culture. Using every available medium, we've succeeded in connecting those hungry for ideas and information to those putting them into practice.

Friends of PM allows you to directly help impact, amplify, and revitalize the discourse and actions of radical writers, filmmakers, and artists. It provides us with a stable foundation from which we can build upon our early successes and provides a much-needed subsidy for the materials that can't necessarily pay their own way. You can help make that happen—and receive every new title automatically delivered to your door once a month—by joining as a Friend of PM Press. And, we'll throw in a free T-shirt when you sign up.

Here are your options:

- **$30 a month**: Get all books and pamphlets plus 50% discount on all webstore purchases
- **$40 a month**: Get all PM Press releases (including CDs and DVDs) plus 50% discount on all webstore purchases
- **$100 a month**: Superstar—Everything plus PM merchandise, free downloads, and 50% discount on all webstore purchases

For those who can't afford $30 or more a month, we're introducing **Sustainer Rates** at $15, $10 and $5. Sustainers get a free PM Press T-shirt and a 50% discount on all purchases from our website.

Your Visa or Mastercard will be billed once a month, until you tell us to stop. Or until our efforts succeed in bringing the revolution around. Or the financial meltdown of Capital makes plastic redundant. Whichever comes first.

ABOUT PM PRESS

PM Press was founded at the end of 2007 by a small collection of folks with decades of publishing, media, and organizing experience. PM Press co-conspirators have published and distributed hundreds of books, pamphlets, CDs, and DVDs. Members of PM have founded enduring book fairs, spearheaded victorious tenant organizing campaigns, and worked closely with bookstores, academic conferences, and even rock bands to deliver political and challenging ideas to all walks of life. We're old enough to know what we're doing and young enough to know what's at stake.

We seek to create radical and stimulating fiction and nonfiction books, pamphlets, T-shirts, visual and audio materials to entertain, educate, and inspire you. We aim to distribute these through every available channel with every available technology, whether that means you are seeing anarchist classics at our bookfair stalls; reading our latest vegan cookbook at the café; downloading geeky fiction e-books; or digging new music and timely videos from our website.

Contact us for direct ordering and questions about all PM Press releases, as well as manuscript submissions, review copy requests, foreign rights sales, author interviews, to book an author for an event, and to have PM Press attend your bookfair:

PM Press • PO Box 23912 • Oakland, CA 94623
510-658-3906 • info@pmpress.org
Buy books and stay on top of what we are doing at:
www.pmpress.org

ABOUT REACH AND TEACH

Reach And Teach is a peace and social justice learning company, transforming the world through teachable moments. They publish and distribute books, music, posters, games, curriculum, and DVDs that focus on peacemaking and healing the planet.

Reach And Teach
144 W. 25th Ave.
San Mateo, CA 94403
www.reachandteach.com